ARE WE FRIENDS NOW?

AN ANTHOLOGY BY AND ABOUT
2SLGBTQ+ YOUTH FROM PEI

ACORNPRESS

Editor: Tom Ryan
Cover art: Katie Perry
Interior: Tracy Belsher

Printed in Canada

Library and Archives Canada Cataloguing in Publication

Title: Are we friends now? / an anthology by and about 2SLGBTQ+ youth from PEI.
Names: Ryan, Tom, 1977 February 26- editor. | PEI Writers' Guild, publisher. | PEERS
Alliance (Firm), publisher. Description: Edited by Tom Ryan. | Co-published by PEI
Writers' Guild and PEERS Alliance. Identifiers: Canadiana (print) 20230476368 |
Canadiana (ebook) 20230476376 | ISBN 9781773661407 (softcover) | ISBN
9781773661414 (EPUB) Subjects: LCSH: Sexual minorities' writings, Canadian. |
LCSH: Youths' writings, Canadian. | LCSH: Sexual minority youth—Prince Edward
Island—Literary collections. | LCSH: Homosexuality—Prince Edward Island—Literary
collections. | CSH: Canadian literature (English)—21st century. | LCGFT: Literature.
Classification: LCC PS8637.H67 A74 2023 | DDC C813/.608035266—dc23

Canadä   Canada Council
for the Arts   Conseil des Arts
du Canada

The publisher acknowledges the support of the Government of Canada, the

Canada Council for the Arts and the Province of Prince Edward Island for our

publishing program.

ACORNPRESS

P.O. Box 22024
Charlottetown, Prince Edward Island
C1A 9J2
acornpresscanada.com

INTRODUCTION
Tom Ryan, Editor (he/him)

Last November, I drove from Cape Breton to Charlottetown to meet with a group of talented young writers at the PEI Writers' Guild and PEERS Alliance Queer Youth Writing Club. We spent a lively evening brainstorming ideas for this anthology, and I returned home the next day infected by the group's enthusiasm, and energized and excited about the work that lay ahead of us.

In the months since, I've worked closely with these young writers and their adult facilitators to help them develop their work for this collection. Working with PEERS Alliance, the PEI Writers' Guild and their many volunteers has been a wonderful experience, but it's the young writers and their beautiful words that really make this anthology shine. I'm so proud of everyone who contributed, and excited for those of you who are about to experience it for the first time.

When I was still in high school, safe spaces like this were non-existent, and this kind of project would have been unthinkable. There's no question that young people are feeling more empowered to present their true selves to the world than ever, but this progress comes in the face of an alarming pushback against LGBTQ+ rights. I feel strongly that the best way to fight back against this kind of harmful and intimidating rhetoric is by raising our voices and sharing our stories, which is why a collection like this one is so powerful and important. I'm honoured to have worked on it.

We hope you enjoy it.

FOREWORD:
THiS iS THE ONLY PLACE i CAN BE MYSELF
Vanessa Bradley (she/her), PEERS Alliance

There is so much joy to be found in queerness and community. Watching the youth of the Queer Writing Club build that community and find support for each other has been a great privilege.

In January of 2022, I met with Shawn Hogan (he/him) of the PEI Writers' Guild to discuss the possibility of partnering on a project. Within a week, we were planning to write a grant to get funds for a queer youth writing club that would also publish participant writing in an anthology.

The PEI Alliance for Mental Well-Being awarded us the grant! We are absolutely ecstatic to have brought a writing club for queer youth to life in Prince Edward Island. Our goal with creating the writing club was to improve mental health among our participants and help them develop resiliency. We went into this project knowing the importance of community as it relates to writing (so often a solo act!), but we certainly did not expect all of the beauty that would come about as a result.

We watched as young people who were initially hesitant to share received support and kept sharing. We listened to plot ideas and the beginnings of poems. Self-deprecating comments were met with a chorus of "no negative self-talk", a community guideline established at the beginning of the writing club. We watched as snacks were eaten and inside jokes were shared. When a youth changed their name, the others never skipped a beat. Participants who had been hesitant to share their opinions and disagree with others began to calmly state their opinions (one youth said "We have a different experience of that but I respect your point" and both Shawn and I cheered internally). They learned how to lean into themselves and their writing. Together, they built a community.

An incredible part of this project has simply been watching members of the group take one another's writing seriously. Writing is something that is so vulnerable and personal, and many studies have shown how much writing helps promote mental resilience, improve mental health, and enhance mental well-being—and what we have also seen first-hand is how essential this kind of community can be to the experience.

To be able to have a place where youth can come, be themselves, learn with their peers, and gain wisdom and insight from adults in the 2SLGBTQ+ community who are thriving as writers is nothing short of a gift. And then to have a talented author, Tom Ryan, edit the youth's writing, express genuine interest and excitement over their work, and help them hone their words into something even better was a dream from start to finish. The youth were so excited at getting their words published and into this beautiful book you're holding in your hands.

My personal favourite part? Seeing the look on their faces when they talked about their chosen names, in print with their words beneath it, published in a book.

We hope that you enjoy these stories from 2SLGBTQ+ youth and that you see the love and joy and community (and angst) that's been poured into this book.

Support programs like these!
Support 2SLGBTQ+ youth by donating to PEERS Alliance at
www.peersalliance.ca
Support the writing community on the island by donating to the
PEI Writers' Guild at www.peiwritersguild.com

CHARLiE'S 18TH BiRTHDAY

Roisin Mullen (she/he/they)
(CW: threat of violence)

"Happy Birthday dear Charlie, Happy Birthday to you!" Charlie's mother finished singing and he blew out the candles on top of his cake.

Today was a bittersweet day because today was the day Charlie turned 18. And in this day and age, sometime after you turn 18 you get that dreaded knock on the door and you either have to reveal your deepest darkest secret on live TV for all the world to hear or you get shot in the head.

Charlie's mother reached across the table and brushed her hand against his.

"I know what you're thinking." Charlie looked up and locked eyes with his mother. "There's no telling when they'll come. I didn't have to spill the beans until I was in my mid-twenties. You never know, you could live your whole life without seeing them, then when you're old and on your death bed they come into your hospital room. That's what happened to John's father, remember?"

Of course he remembered. It was one of the first confessions he remembered seeing of someone he knew.

"Why do they even have to do that? Why can't we just live our lives?"

"It's to keep us honest. Besides, you must have to do something really bad to rather die than confess. It gets rid of the worst of us."

Charlie was silent. His mother wasn't technically wrong but Charlie didn't want to believe that she was right.

There was a knock at the door.

Charlie stood up and put his chair between him and the door.

"Don't worry Charlie, it's only your uncle Emmett. He just got into town last night so I invited him for cake."

His mother made her way to the door and opened it.

"Emmett! So lovely to ..." She froze. Two masked people barged into the room, one holding a gun, one holding a camera.

"No please, no!" Charlie screamed.

One of the masked people grabbed Charlie, threw him onto the chair and put their gun to his head. The other masked person set up the camera facing him.

"Confess now or die," said the one with the gun, in a voice that was altered to be neither masculine or feminine.

"No! Please! I'd rather die."

"Charlie please!" His mother started crying. "I don't care what you did, I can't live without you!" She fell down on her knees.

"I can't live with that information in the world." Charlie started to cry. "What if I lose my job? What if no one is willing to date me? I'll be alone forever!"

"I would never leave you," she said. "Nothing you could ever say would make me want to leave you!"

"You wouldn't love me if you found out!"

"Yes I would!"

"No you wouldn't!"

"Yes! I would!"

"No!"

"Yes! Please, just tell them!"

"Fine!" Charlie took a deep breath to compose himself. He looked up at the camera "When I was little at my grandparents' house ..." He paused and took in a shaky breath. "They had one of those old tv's ... You know the kind that looks like a box with the little antenna on it?" Charlie looked at his mother, and she nodded encouragingly.

"Well... I licked it." Charlie looked down at his feet in shame.

"What?" His mother was puzzled. "What do you mean you licked it?"

"When Grammy and Grampa left the room ... sometimes I would switch the channel so it was staticky, and it felt fuzzy on my fingers so I licked it." Charlie started crying again.

"Are you shitting me? That's your secret?"

"I knew you wouldn't love me ... I'm a failure."

His mother shook her head in disbelief. "I still love you Charlie but sometimes you can be quite the drama queen."

"Wait a minute," said the person with the gun. "That was your secret? I don't get paid enough for this shit."

The masked person with the camera started taking it down. "Are we still good to get pizza?" he asked the masked person with the gun.

"Most definitely."

AND THE WOODEN DUCK FLIES

Seth C.G. (he/him)

Hello
It's been a week

I etched your name
In every crevice I could find
And every place I could imagine
So I may never forget you

Your ashes remain in my treasure chest
Locked deep away
But not too deep
So that one day
When I am lonely and grieving
I can bring you back to life
For just a moment

I carved your name into a wooden duck
And let you fly free
Floating down the river with glee
But the next day you came back
Tattered and chewed
So I decided to keep you around for a while longer

But you are a wooden duck
And can not talk to me
And can not speak to me
But whenever I let you go I can't
Help but feel like you're still there
As a ghost
Watching over my every move

I think there's so many things
I wish I could've told you
But never did
And I regret never telling you
My good things
Or my bad things
Because you would always listen

You would always listen to me
Listen to me be happy
Listen to me be sad
Listen to me be me
You loved me

You always told me
You would always watch me
From heaven
And honestly

I do believe it
Because now
Everything I do
Feels like I'm being watched over

And maybe that's not a bad thing
But I can't escape you
Even when I try really hard

Because you were me
You were just as much me as I was you
And now you're a wooden duck
Ghosting my life
Following my every move

Your cold phantom
Lies its sunny fingertips around my shoulders
But you aren't there
Because you are a wooden duck
And I am a human

I think you may regain your wings
And fly towards the heavens
But until then
You are always welcome with me
The wooden duck I carry

That's all I have to say today
I'll be back next week
Goodbye
I love you

UNTiTLED

Mnemosyne Tabangin (she/they)

I hate my job.

As I sit here, under the tapestry of the night, hidden in the shadows of the alleyway, I hate myself. It's a common feeling, in all honesty. I mean, don't you ever just curse yourself out?

My breathing is heavy yet shallow, my arms and legs quaking from sprinting through the streets, my pure silver basket fallen on the ground.

Oh, you're a monster hunter? Where's your weapon? Listen, the basket WAS my weapon, ok? I will not elaborate.

I should probably explain more stuff about me. My name, blah blah, but I'm honestly quaking in my boots, too stuttered to even think straight as I keep mumbling on.

How am I still alive? Good question. I don't know.

It's more embarrassing that I'm acting like this despite being history's most acclaimed monster hunter of all time. My name is in books, and I can't even remember it, how pathetic.

I shudder and let out another breath, my shaking hands reaching to grab the handle of my basket. The monster I was hunting is now in pursuit of me, and I brought them here into the city. I'm so stupid.

My hands shake more as they grip harder onto the cold metal, my eyes staring down at the rather childish weapon, my own misty reflection scratched and dull from the texturing. My yellow eyes look tired and scared, as usual, weary from almost everything. I truly am a coward, but that never really makes me sad as it is just true. I am very insecure, but I'm never fully sad? Depressed? Off topic again. Sigh.

My eyes widen as my hearing focuses on a point. Whatever noise there was is gone, my head filled with pure nothingness other than a small, tiny hum. My body tenses, the hum getting louder.

(to be continued...)

ARE WE FRiENDS NOW?

POEM #1

Elizabeth Morrison (she/her)

He is everything I was not.

He is refined, where I was raw.

He is sharp, where I was malleable.

He is stable, where I was delicate.

He is mild, where I was adamant.

He is the quenching lake on the most stifling of summer
days.

He is the fingers interlocking with your own, ne'er a bead of sweat
between your palms.

He is the familiar ease of reading your dearest book once more.

He is the melting of snow after the blistering days of winter.

Or... he is not.

He must be all of those things, and more.

He must be.

He must be each and every one of those things, for he deserved the
parts of you that I did not.

He is not yours clandestinely, cherished only behind closed doors,
the way I once was.

He is not the one whom you could never kiss, trapped in the grasp
of your dread to desire.

He is not I, for He is not a She.

I sought after his qualities upon which you bestowed worth,

I recreated my individuality, fixed on becoming someone onto whom you could grant your affection.

I refined where I once was raw.

I sharpened where I once was malleable.

I became stable where I once was delicate.

I became mild, when my soul howled to be adamant.

But, I could never be the quenching lake, the dry palms, the familiar ease, nor the melting snow.

For I am not He.

I am rays of sunlight that once warmed your velvet skin.

I am artless limbs entangled with your own, encased in the shelter of darkness.

I am frigid bones beneath the hug of a calescent hearth.

I am the leaves of autumn entombed beneath the flakes of spiteful snow.

Or... I am not.

I had been indoctrinated into assuming the identity of He whom you decided to worship.

I was indeterminately absorbed in my desire to once again be the recipient of your affection.

In the encapsulating haze of such desire, I irrevocably relinquished my soul.

I am not He.

But... since you, my love, I am no longer She.

EXCERPT FROM "FOX"

Hayden Little (she/her)

Being chased is so very exciting. The way they shout "Elizabeth! Elizabeth!" reminds me of a swarm of insects.

My skirts curled through my fingers as I tore through the afternoon sun- it's where they liked to sit when I'm being wicked. I needed the space between the long fabric and my boots so as not to trip, the heels were bothersome enough—I would have taken them off long ago if I wasn't in such a dreadful hurry. And yet despite my determination I knew I wasn't moving quick enough, because as I dove into the orchard Helen jumped in my path. No matter, she didn't reach me in time.

I veered swiftly into the trees, weaving my way through their generous spacing until I burst out into the field. Sparing no glance back I ran, ran until my breaths were ragged and my lungs begged for pause. It felt like a game, this, one I quite enjoyed. It wasn't like chess, more like the games of tag I played with Caroline before she declared us too old for it. The one problem was I wasn't looking where I was going, so when I tripped I did not expect it.

My body went tumbling as did my mind, right until they both slammed into the trunk of a tree. I rose dizzily and with pain everywhere at once, covered in dirt and rips which I chose to pay less attention to when I realized the trouble I'd surely be in.

The forest on the edge of my father's land has been forbidden since my birth, and this was the first time I had witnessed it. The afternoon sun made it look devastatingly heavenly, with amber-spotted grass and flowers whose petals were thrown open in embrace. It was a sight so beautiful that it wrenched savagely at my heart. I extended my fingers to caress the dress of a wildflower, cupping its colorful bodice in the palm of my hand like a duckling. It swooned in my hold and lay gazing up at me curiously and we remained this way until an unusual ringing broke the silence.

I startled up and looked around, tearing the flower from the earth in the process. The source was perched on a branch behind me, gazing down like he'd just woken from a deep sleep. He was dressed in odd finery, a tailcoat green as grass with dark embroidered thorns and ivy down the front, untouched by dirt or muck except for the heels of his boots. On his brow sat a circlet of bluebells, ones that rang just like bells when he tilted his head to catch my eye, and upon doing so he did the strangest thing: he smiled. But the odd thing about this gesture was not the gesture itself, it was the way he presented it. It was the most foxlike grin I'd ever seen, wide and gentle with a tricky curl at both ends.

Everything about him was strange, foreign and new and I felt drawn to him at once. I unhinged my jaw to speak and was interrupted before I could utter a syllable by the sound of Caroline shouting my name.

It felt like I'd been hauled out from an icy wave I hadn't even noticed being under. My sense shouted at me and, scrambling to my feet, I turned and rushed up the path without looking back. When I emerged from the mouth of the forest I saw my dearest friend wringing her hands in the field. I suppose Helen knew she was the only one who could successfully lure me out of hiding, thankfully for them she lived close to father's estate. Caroline sucked in a breath to call again, though stopped herself when she caught sight of me and instead swiftly made her way over.

"Oh Elizabeth, what a mess you've made of yourself." Caroline's delicate lips turned down in what could have been concern while plucking a twig out of my hair.

Despite my previous shock I smiled. "I didn't mean to this time." I assured her, but she looked at me like I'd just said something very foolish.

"You hadn't resolved to hide from your guest in the forest you've been very clearly forbidden from?" Caroline asked, but it wasn't a question. I pushed the encounter I'd had from my mind and decided upon looking away shamefully. I didn't feel ready to share the strange boy with the bluebell crown I'd seen with her, not yet at least. Caroline expected a confession, but when I didn't offer one she sighed and together we returned to the estate. Upon entrance Caroline began to usher me down the hall insisting I wash up, but I knew she wished to guide me past the drawing room before I made any more ruckus.

Unfortunately for her the newest suitor my father had invited, Mr. Thompson, was leaving as we passed by. When our eyes met I made sure to smile as wildly as possible, hoping to drive him off by making him believe he'd be marrying an animal and not a girl. I believe it worked, but I was handed to Helen and dragged to my rooms before I could truly admire the results.

Helen was cross with me, no pleased woman could've scrubbed my scalp so violently if not, even if it did work. Once the water was murky and I was clean I dressed in a new gown and rushed downstairs to find Caroline and invite her to stay for supper. Father hasn't ever minded Caroline's company, she's much more polite and proper than I, we assume that he believes it will rub off on me. I took no more than two paces down the hall when I saw my father, his expression grim. He gestured to me and I tailed him into the drawing room, spotting an untouched teapot and chairs. He sank into one and gestured to the other, but I remained standing.

"My daughter, my only daughter, I urge you to see what I see." Father sighed. "I am growing old, and should you continue refusing suitors there will be no one to inherit the land."

"I do not wish for a husband." I countered. "If I had one I would weep day and night of bitterness. To be wed is to be shackled to a wholly uncertain future. I myself could run the estate, if only you'd let me."

"It is not your place to run the estate, you wouldn't be able." We've spoken of this before." He looked tired already.

"Not now perhaps, but given the proper lessons I'm certain I could run it marvelously." I replied.

"You would not pay attention to those studies, you hardly pay attention to your own." Father said. "Should I foolishly hand you that responsibility, the estate would fall. You require a man who will keep things running."

"Perhaps my studies aren't what I excel at." I retorted. "I shall play the role of a widow to inherit the land if I must, I will not marry." I expected to be shouted at or the like, but father just leaned back in his chair with an exasperated sigh. I left him then, finding Caroline waiting in the hall.

We strolled out into the orchard, each choosing an apple fallen from branches to give one another.

"Why were you in the forest?" Caroline asked once we were flanked by apple trees.

"I tripped and fell, the sticks in my hair should be proof enough of that. I meant only to hide until Mr Thompson took his leave." It had been my original plan to find somewhere to hide, but Helen and the other servants had thrown a wrench in it, not that I hadn't enjoyed running from them.

"You'd give Mr. Wood more gray hairs than before if he caught wind of this, you know."

I shot her a startled look. "You wouldn't tell my father."

"I wasn't planning to. I shouldn't like to upset him, either." Caroline admitted, turning her apple gingerly in her hands while I bit into mine.

"His reason is no likely one, I've never understood it."

"You need not understand it," Said she. "Just obey for his peace of mind, it's the least you can do for the trouble you bring."

"You'll stay for supper, won't you?" I decided to cut the conversation short and Caroline noticed, though questioned not.

"If you'll have me." She answered, polite as ever. Despite it we smiled together.

⁓

Caroline visited so often she was considered a resident of the estate, so my father cast no second glance as we two entered the dining room and seated ourselves. But the maids did, since they had to bring out another plate.

"What a fine evening it is, Mr. Wood." Caroline said.

"Indeed." He drawled. I could tell, with an inner wince, that he still hadn't recovered from our quarrel. Father pinched the bridge of his nose before looking up with a more pleasant face to lighten the mood. "How have you been, Miss Evans?"

"Oh very well, thank you." Caroline replied, attempting to hide the excitement in her voice, one that made me lean forward in interest. "This morning I received an invitation to the ball that Count Wick is organizing in three weeks time."

"How wonderful! And what a coincidence, too. An invitation arrived for Elizabeth this afternoon."

I whirled on my father at this news. "What?" I demand. "When?"

"When Helen was retrieving you, Elizabeth." He answered lightly. Ah, when I was being chased.

"We will see each other there then." Caroline smiled, but I could see the silent pleading in her eyes, begging I not cause a ruckus. I couldn't promise anything, while I could try, it has always been in my nature to cause trouble.

"Is there anyone you hope to meet at the ball?" I asked Caroline, referring to any certain man. Unlike myself, Caroline had always wished to marry and have a family, she often had her eyes on at least one man, and when her cheeks took on a pink shade I knew that was the reason she was so thrilled. Caroline may come off as very well mannered and rational on the outside, but she was just a girl swooning for boys inside. I had no doubt she would find one, either. She's very beautiful, with flowing curls of straw and eyes of earth. I've thought to myself countless times that, should I ever choose one to marry, it would be her.

While we talked over supper, inside I felt shocked by Caroline's skill at easing us both. I'd hardly even noticed the tension in the air until she'd woven me out of it. I suppose just her company was enough. Since my birth and the loss of my mother, Helen tells me it's been significantly quieter. Caroline is like a beam of sunlight in a dimly lit room, warming us all with talk of her family and social life. She told us of how William, her youngest brother, had tamed a goose with berries while the nanny wasn't looking. Presently it came to the garden every morning to meet with him, no matter how much the maids tried to shoo it off. The story was warm and childish, and by the time supper had come to a close and Caroline was readying herself to return home our minds were eased. That was, until I retired to my rooms.

I'd left the wildflower I had torn from the forest ground by the windowsill, and after dressing in my nightclothes I climbed on the sill and cradled it in my hands. Its dress was curling in on itself, being without resources for too long. I knew I could not save it and so did not try, just observed it and then the outside of my window.

The forest has always looked like a cupped hand to me, curling round the edge of my father's land and extending like an arm beyond it. Inside it somewhere was the tree he had sat upon, that strange, unbelievable boy with the fox grin. He was no suitor, that I knew for certain, but if not a suitor then who? A wanderer perhaps. Or a witch. Who else could have made a crown of flowers that sang like bells? Oddly enough, the thought didn't scare me. He didn't scare me. But he did spark my curiosity. I drifted to sleep with the thought of seeing him again, of speaking with him, of returning to the forest.

When I awoke the next morning the sun had barely risen. My face was pressed against the window, creating not the most charming sight to any who might've seen me, but I welcomed a sight like that, it scared the men away.

I enjoy the early mornings, it makes one feel as if they're the only person alive, no matter where they go. But this morning was an exception, since as I stood and made my way to my dresser I stopped myself. On my bed untouched and neat sat an astilbe. The flower looked like it had been plucked very precisely from the earth.

ZINNIAS

(one of a series of flower coded poems)
Anaclara Leyenaar (she/they)

In wormwood of your life
My heart will heal with Aloe and thyme
Your wormwood from my heart needs comfrey
For rosemary will be St John's wort.
To chickweed the white willow
Will Raspberry to oats
For the California Poppy cannot be.

(Poem decoded)

In absence of your life
My heart will heal with pain and fortitude
Your absence from my heart will need mending
For remembrance will be the light in the darkness
To start fresh the ways of water
Will create space to just be
For resurrection cannot be.

WAX WINGS

Seth C.G. (he/him)

Though your wings were made to melt in the heat,
I noticed that your soul was not ready,
Though you claimed that you just could not be beat,
You failed the test of will to hold steady,

You were made of crystals, and clean, pure wax,
And I suppose you could've been just great,
But you lacked strength, you were just too laid back,
So that is why you are known as The Late,

When you flew up, too high, too close, sweating,
You drowned in the radiance of the light,
My lessons, I knew you were forgetting,
And suddenly, your world was filled with blight,

In lieu of this, you still are my best friend,
But together, I wish we saw the end.

THE LOG

River Waterman (they/them)

Resting unburdened,
untroubled,
sound and silent, an eternity
bound in this moment,
this log, this space
that is empty, not
an air full of
uncomfortable polka dots
and yellow squeezing
at your thoughts.
The log is simple,
encompassing everything
in passive silence,
as though the world
is holding your breath
and its ears are full of
water and birdsong. As though
the log is thinking for you,
in tones of brown and
night sky with no stars,
as though
all of existence is turned to

fog and condensed, only
to form the breath
of a lone
water strider.

BETTER BADGES

Tanya Davis, Queer Youth Writing Club Facilitator (she/her)

The orientation badge, for getting lost and then finding ourselves, again and again

The backpacking badge, for packing back and forth across unfamiliar territory

The discovering faith badge, for making it through bible camp and rising again

The stargazer badge, for imagining another world is possible

The biology badge, for quivering with wild beings and seeing that we, like all animals, just want to be free

The animal husbandry badge, for learning that not all animals need husbands

The inventor's badge, for experimenting with different ways to be

The dropping-out-of-girl-guides badge, because the badges were boring and we wanted to create something but were only rewarded for mending it

The badge for emergency preparedness, because all queers get one

The archaeology badge, for digging down deep to find love we couldn't see on the surface

The archery badge, for not assuming who is on what side of a straight arrow or that there are sides in the first place

The communication badge, for all the conversations with strangers and family, to undo assumptions and work for understanding

The family care badge, for caring for our chosen families even if their blood ones couldn't, or didn't. Also, for forgiving blood and chosen families for their ignorance

The construction badge, for not being taught how to build things because we were supposed to find "a man" to operate the tools

The tools badge, because fuck that

The journalism badge, for asking important questions

The law badge, for calling authority into question

The sustainability badge, for sustaining love in a society that would see ours suffer

The wilderness survival badge, because it is a wild world, and we survive it together.

LOST iN THE UNiVERSE

Anaclara Leyenaar (she/they)

(CW: physical and emotional abuse and alcohol abuse)

Not a true story.

Universe

Universe: the whole cosmic system of matter and energy of which Earth, and therefore the human race, is a part.

Ivy

I'm running. Always running. From him, me and the universe. I live with my Uncle Phil and he drinks too much. He always hallucinates when he is drunk. Every time he does this, I run away, try and get away from him and he always chases me, calling me, yelling, "Margaret, Margaret! Come here you little monster."

First, that's my dead name. My name is Ivy. And secondly, I'm not little, I'm thirteen. Also, it might sound cute when he yells that, like he cares, but I know he doesn't. I usually go to the 45 coffee shop in downtown Hamilton when he's drunk. The people there are nice to me. They take care of me. Almost like family, but my family is gone. It fell apart years ago. Ever since my parents died when I was 9, I've had to stay with Phil (just saying his name makes me want to gag.) I don't like staying with him, but I have to. He's my legal guardian, the only family I have left. I have cuts, bruises and scars. I try to hide them with long sleeves and my favorite red sunglasses, but it's hard.

Often when people see me, they assume I'm a delinquent who is constantly getting into fights. I wish I could be a normal kid with kind, loving and accepting parents, but the universe doesn't think I deserve to be happy. So this is my life; dead parents, a drunk uncle and a house where I never feel safe.

Home

Home: the house or flat that you live in, especially with your family.

Hideaway

I don't go to school. I don't know how to read very well and I hate public school. I just roam the streets downtown. When Uncle Phil is drunk, I hide. I go back for dinner and to sleep, but that's not my home. When I entered the house today, he was taking out a bottle of wine.

"I think you should put away the bottle, you don't need it right now," I said.

Out of nowhere, he grabbed my wrist and yelled at me. "You can't tell me what to do. I'm in charge here and next time you sneak out or say something out of order your wrist will be broken!"

"O-okay," I said with a quiver in my voice. I knew I shouldn't have said a word, but I also knew that he would chase me again. I ate quickly and went to bed, locking my door before he had too much wine.

Around 10 pm, I heard him stumbling up the stairs to my room. I'm always terrified when I'm near him. He knocked on my door until around midnight, yelling and cursing until I heard him fall asleep. I don't ever fall asleep till I'm sure he's out cold, then and only then will I drift off to a restless night of phantoms and terrors.

Fear

Fear: the bad feeling that you have when you are in danger or when a particular thing frightens you.

The Hospital

The next morning, I woke up around 5:30 to Uncle Phil sleeping at my door. The wine was probably out of his system, but I wasn't sure. I tried to sneak out of the house but he snuck up behind me and caught my wrist before I could go through the front door.

"You know what I said includes you not sneaking out," he said, slurring his words a bit. He was hungover like every other day. I knew he was going to do it before he did it. I saw the pain before it hit me. Then he let go and I ran as fast as I could. The pain of my broken wrist drove me as I ran to the coffee shop.

As soon as I got there, they called an ambulance. They took me to the hospital as fast as they could. I didn't want them to touch me, but I was in so much pain that I let them. After I got to the hospital, it was all a blur. I remember the doctors brought me to get an x-ray, then they took me to get a cast. I remember waking up in a hospital bed, tired, scared and confused.

A doctor came and started to talk to me.

"Hi Margaret, my name is Dr. Kelly and I'd like to ask you a few questions. Is that okay?"

"Yes, but you have to call me by my name. That's my dead name. My name is Ivy."

"OK Ivy, my first question is, how did you break your wrist? It looks like someone twisted it."

I decided that I would tell her everything.

"When my parents died I went to live with my Uncle Phil, but he got into a bad habit of drinking."

"Did he break your wrist?" she asked.

"Yes," I said, looking down. I didn't like him, but he was still technically family.

"Okay. Well, you know you can't stay with him."

"I don't want to stay with him," I yelled. "I'm scared when I'm with him," I confessed in a softer voice.

"I'm going to have to call social services and see what's going to happen to your uncle."

I was silent for a few minutes, then I asked her, "what will happen to me?"

"You will go to a foster home and hopefully get adopted," Dr. Kelly said. She started to walk out of the room and then turned back to me. "There are some nice people who you will be living with. They will be your foster family."

Belonging

Belonging: the feeling of being comfortable and happy in a particular situation or with a particular group of people, and being treated as a full member of the group.

Alexandria, Elizabeth & Benjamin

My foster parents' names are Alexandria (I call her Alex) and Elizabeth (I call her Lizzy). My foster brother's name is Benjamin (I've nicknamed him Benny). Alex is tall and has nice curly red-brown hair, Lizzy is shorter than Alex and has short dark brown hair, Benny is 10 and also has curly red-brown hair. They were nice to me. They bought me a nice green dress, some black leggings, and some nice jeans. They didn't have any alcohol in the house, no beer, wine or whiskey. They were very kind and considerate of my feelings. I wasn't scared when I was with them. I knew they loved me as if I was their own daughter/sister. I didn't like them touching me much. I didn't want to love them because I knew the universe would kick me all over again like it did when my parents died. I mostly stayed in my new bedroom, all painted blue. We would play fun board games at the dining room table when I wasn't in my bedroom.

On Monday, Alex asked me something that I didn't want to hear. "Do you want to go to public school or do you want us to homeschool you?"

"I am not going to public school!" I yelled defiantly. I hated that place. All the kids with their parents. It was torture.

"Well, do you want to try Homeschooling?" Lizzy asked me. "Um... okay." I said, not sure what I was going to be doing.

Growth

Growth: An increase in the size or the importance of something.

Homeschooling

Homeschooling was fun. Benny also started homeschooling with me. Alex taught us math, music, and geography. Elizabeth taught us history, science, literature and she taught me how to read. I was so happy learning with them. I loved geography, it was my favorite subject. For geography, every Wednesday we would go for a hike and every time we would go to a different place. Once we went to Niagara Falls, and had a lovely picnic there. Math was my second favorite subject. Then literature because I got to write short stories! I loved playing the piano with Alex. She was a great piano teacher. The old piano was so fun to play songs on. The music always danced in the room around us when we were playing. I learned 'Twinkle, Twinkle Little Star', 'Happy Birthday', and once I was good enough I learned how to play some more advanced music, like 'Ode to Joy' by Beethoven and 'Can you Read my Mind' by John Williams. I've been running for so long I'm almost afraid to slow down.

Family

Family: a group of persons united by the ties of marriage, blood, or adoption, constituting a single household and interacting with each other in their respective social positions, usually those of spouses, parents, children, and siblings.

Adopted

I have been living with my new family for 6 months. The day had finally come and today they were going to adopt me! It had been tough at times, but after a few months they truly became my new family. Alexandria and Elizabeth are awesome moms and Benjamin is a great little brother. I am so excited for them to be my new family, kind and loving. We drove to City Hall in our cobalt blue Volkswagen camper bus we call Bell and we went into the courtroom. It was small, but intimidating with red carpeted flooring and old dark wood benches. It reminded me of the church I went to with my parents when they were alive. We sat down and talked to the judge. All the papers got signed. I have a new family now, but I will never forget the past. On the drive home to celebrate, we picked up a delicious DQ Oreo ice cream cake that read in chocolate icing writing "Welcome 2 the fam".

TO THE SHOOTING STAR

Seth C.G. (he/him)

Oh shooting star,

How much longer must I wait,
Before I become one with you?

Before our souls unite,
And we sing our harmonies,
Sing our stories in great visions,
For the world to hear forever.

Oh shooting star,

How much longer must I wait,
Before I can dance with you?

So we can show each other,
Where we came from,
And find the answers,
To where we all come from.

Oh shooting star,

How much longer must I wait,
Before I become a star myself?

Every day I seem,
To wait for a day that never comes,
And sometimes the waiting,
It just feels so pointless.

Oh shooting star,

How much longer must I wait,
Before I see you again?

To see your beauty,
You bless the sky with your presence,
And turn a once empty world,
Into a whole new galaxy for us to explore.

QUEER VIEW MIRROR

Dave Stewart, Queer Youth Writing Club Facilitator (he/him)

I knew that I was a boy who liked boys when I was six years old. I also knew, instinctively, that it was not okay to be that kind of boy. Everything in the world around me in the 1970s told me so. People like me were a punchline, a threat, a victim, a tragic character in a movie.

Regardless of how negative representation was at that time, I sought it out. After all, visibility is visibility, and I desperately wanted — *needed* — to know that there were others like me out there somewhere. Sadly, I rarely related to any of the examples available to me, and what I took away from the negative representations and from what my environment was telling me, was that there was no place for a kid like me.

So, what becomes of the shy boy with creative leanings who doesn't like sports? Does he just fade away?

In my case, yes, I thought that fading away was the only course of action to take. Not in the physical sense, mind you, but in terms of destroying the person I was. What I needed was to re-emerge from the ashes, some sort of straight phoenix, reborn and righted.

So I began. I studied straight boys in school. I watched how they walked, I listened to how they talked, and I made sure to mimic them as best I could. Suppressing myself, becoming a chameleon was a matter of survival. It was as exhausting as it was soul crushing. It was also a facade I continued until my early thirties. At its core, it was a lie. Eventually, it proved to be a lie that was impossible to maintain.

It wasn't all so emotionally Dickensian, however. At some point I was thrown a lifeline. Something to tide me over until it would be possible for me to come out, until I just couldn't camouflage my queerness any longer. It came in the form of a punk rock band from New York City, from out the underground of the lower east side, out of a club called CBGB. It was a band called Blondie and a song called *Heart of Glass*.

In this band, in this song, I could hear the promise of something bigger and better, I understood the possibility of a place for me. Their lead singer Debbie Harry became the white rabbit to my Alice, leading me to Wonderland in my imagination, in this case New York City and all that this Mecca has always held for numberless boys like me. To this day, I still hear the promise that this song makes. It's not hyperbole to wonder if it saved my life.

Many years later, our world has changed in some regards. I've also changed in many ways. I've come out. I've gotten married. I've explored a number of creative opportunities.

With my past in mind, and with what it's taken to get me where I am today, namely comfortable in my own skin, at some point I decided it was time to give back.

I began digitally recording some of PEI's queer history, I started volunteering with local queer organizations. And here I am, as I write this, volunteering with PEERS Alliance with the goal of helping to facilitate the work of young queer writers.

That first day we gathered as the Queer Youth Writing Club, I walked into our room at the Haviland Club and met Vanessa, our fearless and well-loved leader. I met Shawn, an ally and Executive Director of the PEI Writers' Guild, who is partnering with PEERS Alliance on this project. I met some fellow volunteers, but most importantly, I meet the young writers who have filled the pages of this book with their words.

I don't really know what I expected on that first day. For the kids to love me? To be "the cool volunteer"? To find a secret calling?

Whatever it was, I found something more low-key, something more obvious. I found people, young people as unique and as ordinary as anyone else, expressing themselves already with strong indicators of the adults they will soon become. They have their own quirks, their own characters, their own challenges, and their own ways of communicating. This is all reflected in these pages.

Volunteering with this project, I've been able to somewhat assess where queer kids are now, and to compare it to where I was at their age. Trans and non-binary folx are facing the same type of backlash that gay, lesbian and bi people faced when I was a kid. There are still dangers, threats to our very lives posed by ignorance and fuelled by misguided fear. The recent (as of this writing) shooting at Club Q in Colorado makes this painfully clear. But what is different, significantly different, is that now there is a place for queer kids here in little ole PEI, there is an avenue for their voices to be heard. And that very much makes a difference.

What this project and everyone involved with it has proven for me, confirmed for me, was something that Blondie showed me all those years ago. We all deserve a place, and sometimes, for boys like me, kids like this, that place can be found wherever our creative instincts take us. The proof is in the voices transcribed onto these pages. Listen to them. It's the first time they're being heard.

MELLOW MADNESS

Hayden Little (she/her)

Hoozing
Woozing
Swaying like a leaf

Hooded eyes stare
through empty hallucinations
Intoxicated, psychedelic colors
blur his vision of self

'Who am I?'
He asks to nothing
From nothing, whispers cloud his ears
'Who are you?'

'Why I'm god, at least I feel that way'
He replies
downing another swig of poison

EXCERPT FROM UNTITLED WORK

Oak LeBlanc (they/he)

Xavier opened his eyes, unaware of where he was. Looking up, he could tell it was nighttime. He noticed that he didn't have his belongings with him. He sat up and looked around, to see if he could find anything helpful, and noticed he was somewhere surrounded by forest. He then noticed a fairy in front of him.

"Where am I? Who are you, what's going on?" said Xavier, clearly on edge.

"Oh you're awake! I'm Nathan, but most people call me Nate. I was just hanging out, but then I saw you, unconscious, and I didn't want to just leave you so I brought you here instead. Are you okay?"

"You should've just left me there, I would have probably been fine."

"What? Ok, rude. Also, you didn't answer my question, are you okay? You have a pretty big wound on your leg."

"Where is this place?" asked Xavier. "And where's all my stuff?"

"You still didn't answer my question, but this is an area where I just like to hangout! I don't have a map right now, but we're not in fairy or elf territory."

"That is so vague. So you don't have a map? Do you even know where we are?"

"Yes I do," said Nate. "Calm down, geez. I know where we are, I just don't have a map on me right now."

"And my things?"

"Wow, you're so impatient, I took your things because you had an alarming number of weapons, and since our kingdoms are kind of at war I wasn't sure that you wouldn't stab me. I'd rather not take my chances.

"Okay, well can you tell me where you put it?" Xavier was getting frustrated. "I don't know how long I was knocked out, so I should get back."

"Get back? Dude did you not notice the wound on your leg?" Nate pointed at Xavier's leg where there were some blooded bandages. "How did that even happen?"

"I noticed it, but it's fine, I'll just deal with it."

"Deal with it? You can't just deal with it! I may have replaced the bandages on it, you're welcome by the way, but still. That injury is going to take a while to heal on its own."

"It's not like I have a choice!" said Xavier.

"Why not?"

"That's none of your business, so if you don't mind I'll be taking my stuff, and leaving. I have a map in my bag, so you can write where we are, and I can manage from there.

"Fine, if you want to make a dumb decision, then be my guest!"

"Why do you care so much anyway? We literally just met."

"Because I have this thing called empathy, and the ability to not be a jerk."

"Haha, very clever," said Xavier in a completely monotone voice. "Where did you put my stuff?"

"It's just over there," said Nate, pointing.

"Thanks." Xavier got up, and then almost immediately fell to the floor. "Ow! Shit!"

"Oh, does your leg hurt too much to walk it off? Who could've predicted that, I wonder?"

"Mind your own business."

Nate shrugged. "Alright, if that's what you want."

After a good five dedicated minutes of limping and crawling, Xavier, laying on the floor, finally said, "Alright, I give up, I can't walk it off, I admit it. Are you happy?"

"No," said Nate. "I had to watch you try to crawl to your bag with an injured leg, it was sad and disappointing."

"Yeah, well I'm not happy either! I don't know what to do, I can't get home, and my leg hurts like hell! Also it's not like you had to stick around!"

"Alright then, I'll just leave."

"Fine! See if I care."

Nate turned around and started walking away, without a word.

"Okay fine!" yelled Xavier. "I'm sorry. Don't leave, I need your help."

Nate turned to face Xavier.

"Alright, I'll try to help. Let's figure this out, shall we? Okay, you said you had to get somewhere."

"Yes."

"Let's assume the best-case scenario, and say I found you almost immediately, when did you need to be at that place?

Xavier sighed. "Before sunrise."

"Alright, so we still have some time, that's good."

"That's just the best case scenario! It's possible I was knocked out for days."

"Yeah, well," said Nathan. "I'm not the one who's injured so badly that I'm literally laying on the floor because I can't stand up so I get to decide."

"Oh my god," said Xavier, rolling his eyes. "You're insufferable."

"Yeah, well you'd better suffer through it. Like I said, a wound like that is going to take a while to heal on its own, but I might have an idea..."

"Yeah? What is it?"

"Potions," said Nathan, with a big smile.

"What?"

"Potions!"

"I don't know what you're talking about," replied Xavier, completely confused.

"Alright, well I know how to make a mix of plants, and ingredients that will help your wound heal faster."

"So, like medicine? Why didn't you just say medicine?"

"Cuz potion's more awesome!" said Nathan.

"It sounds like a child trying and failing to be cool."

"Exactly, it sounds cooler!"

"Not at all what I meant."

To be continued...

POEM #2
Elizabeth Morrison (she/her)
(CW: school shooting)

tick. tick. tick.
seconds into minutes.
tick. tick. tick.

fingers benumbed.
tick.
body paralyzed.
tick.
prickling tears.
tick. tick. tick.

hurried breaths.
tick.
trembling limbs.
tick.
streaming tears.
tick. tick. tick.

reassuring arms,
gather me near.
tick.
soothing hands,
stroke my hair.

tick.
a quivering voice
whispers "it will be okay."
tick. tick. tick.

the world halts.
tick.
the room unmoving.
tick.
encased in fear.
tick. tick. tick.

a pacifying voice
tick.
lulls once again.
tick.
"I am not going to leave you."
tick. tick. tick.

a robotic voice,
tick.
subsequently reports,
tick.
"The lockdown has ended."
tick. tick. tick.

limbs lock.

tick.
but tender hands return,
tick.
dragging me upright.
tick. tick. tick.

a shielding embrace,
tick.
shelters me from the threat
tick.
while we weep to our cores.
tick. tick. tick.

release.
tick.
vomit.
tick.
unconsciousness takes control.
tick. tick. tick.

echoing we're safe.
tick.
the menace retreated.
tick.
yet trepidation remains.
tick. tick. tick.

days elapse.
tick.
emptiness lingers
tick.
hollowness resides within.
tick. tick. tick.

desolation becomes me.
tick.
nothingness feeds upon me.
tick.
consuming all that I am.
tick. tick. tick.

the emptiness rages,
tick.
forging a war within.
tick.
I submit to its firm grasp.
tick. tick. tick.

I emerge as a husk,
tick.
a shell of my former self.
tick.
unreachable in my plight.
tick. tick. tick.

a slice of light,

emerges through the tenebrosity.

tick.

carving into the greedy flesh,

of the nothingness that consumed me.

tick.

purging myself of its dominance,

unburdening my mind of its impermeable grasp

tick. tick. tick.

tick. tick. tick.

tick. tick.

tick..

JANUARY MORNING SCENE

Molly Williams, Queer Youth Writing Club Facilitator (she/her)

"Robin, time to wake up. First school-day of a new year." Their mother's voice was peace, calming words for what could be a hard day. But maybe things would be different this time. Soon, Robin could find their place.

The dazed fourteen-year-old clasped at the covers, but would be up soon. Julia knew her child well, she didn't criticize Robin for their armour of undone blankets. These would come loose on the nights they tossed-and-turned. Often, they didn't know they were doing it. Something deep within Robin knew supportive shelter was needed, long before their conscience could fear such true feelings away.

There was no sun yet and wouldn't be for an hour at least. Robin always dreaded this. How could waking up this early make sense to any sane person? There had to be some conspiracy, they thought, though there were no theories that seemed even close to less crazy.

Robin had to get up, there was no more fighting that. And Robin was scared to fight. They were always scared no matter which way. They just had to choose the 'least worst' direction and cross their fingers. It was as if Robin was praying that fate knew they wanted good luck, rather than to lie about it. Despite fortune's best attempts, Robin would rarely accept its calls, each was in a language they were never taught. They would beat themself up, constantly. Maybe these mixed signals left fate confused, yielding unsure results for Robin's future attempts at hope. Robin thought they knew what they wanted. They thought this so badly.

There was a light on in the kitchen, though, inviting Robin through their gently opened door. Just before reaching for the knob, they could already smell the pancakes. Julia knew this was Robin's favourite, for mornings and anytime. She wanted Robin to have the best day, so she gave her best too. Whipped cream, strawberries, and all.

"I'm alive..." Robin entered the room with a moan. Their six year-old kitten Sprinkles welcomed the sleepwalker with a soft pass-by caress.

This was their thing. Robin would plop-down on the tile floor, return with pats until Sprinkles rolled onto their back. The type of scritches would vary day-by-day, but would be just as good. Sprinkles and Robin were best friends. Once Robin sat at the counter, Julia also came to life.

"Good morning, kiddo. How was your slumber?"

"So far so good." Robin joked, pretending to continue, dropping a head toward their plate.

"Haha. Bring that humour to school, okay? You sometimes forget it once you leave here."

"I know." Robin said, reserved.

Julia took a moment, starting to check under pancakes. "But it's going to be okay! You're smart and so sweet. Everybody loves that."

"That, I'm not sure..."

"Robin, it's okay to be unsure. I know it hurts, but it's not your fault." The teen looked to Sprinkles while hearing these words. There was so much in that house that Robin loved, that loved Robin.

"I think I'm excited though...? I don't know. I want to be at least."

"Good! That's something," Julia responded. Pancakes began splatting back onto the hot plug-in grill, and she groaned at the sight. Hopefully, she'd get a second chance with a new side. "And remember honey, if today's not easy, we'll be here to catch you once you're home. Your dad and I are both just proud that you're trying to get back to regular school again."

Robin spaced out for a bit. It was one of those conversations that ended naturally, and no one minded. Robin didn't hate talking to their mother, far from that, but sometimes quiet was nice. The radio wasn't even on. Sometimes they would listen to a station together, but Robin would have turned it off today. There was too much to think about, really. Robin always liked to prepare themself the best they could. It was a core part of their identity, for better and for worse.

Julia placed three pancakes on a plate in a pleasing triangle. These were the best-cooked pancakes and had been taken off just in time with care. "To my favorite child," she offered, then bowed.

"Mom, I'm your only child..."

"Competition was fierce in utero! But what am I saying? Would you like strawberries or anything? I even have real whipped cream."

"Ooh, please."

As Julia sliced the berries, Robin buttered each pancake before putting peanut butter on only two. They would often do this. Nothing existential, really, like wanting to know both kinds of 'what could have been'. Robin just liked both and didn't limit themself. They did this with pancakes without a second thought, but struggled to replicate this in life. That's where the existential stuck, for now.

"Thank you so much, Mom. Really. I really appreciate you trying to make things go okay."

"Oh, don't worry about it, sweets! I'm your mom, it's in my job description. Ready?"

The pancakes were exactly what Robin would have hoped for. If today could continue just like this, Robin would be okay. They hoped. Both for a good day, but also to realize it and accept it. Robin never knew what to expect from life, let alone their mind.

They'd joke about losing their mind all the time. Forgetting it like a mitten or a set of headphones. Robin would try their best though. No matter what was given, Robin would survive and live one more time and another time still. They knew that. They wanted to feel it too.

SUNSHOWERS

Hayden Little (she/her)

Extended palms cut through sobbing clouds
spilling out in golden pools
Unveiling marigold spotlights pointed on white skirts
and flowing hair of silk

Rest in my arms tenderly
and soothe me with the soft brush of your lips
Blinded by your lovely warmth
I worship you like none other

Celestial tears soak our skin
above our sun-drenched bodies
But dance, my dear
Let us forget hardship
and sing through lovely sunshowers

WHAT WiLL i LEAVE BEHiND

Seth C.G. (he/him)

There's only so many times,
That I can ponder my own death,
Before it starts to make me think,
I'm going crazy,

I've started seeing visions,
Death, it's dancing,
In the back of my mind I see it,
It's sitting in a chair,
Watching a dusty clock tick,

I think it's counting down,
My last moments, but I,
Can't bring myself to fathom,
That I will die soon,
Because I haven't yet made,
My imprint on the world,

What will I leave behind,
For on this tattered road?

Will my remains remain nothing more,
Than a warning for travellers,
Down this same path as I?

Or will my story be carried,
For generations to come, celebrating me,
Just because I existed?

I could never read,
The hands on that clock,
But I can only assume,
My time is coming soon,
Because every time I see Death,
Its chair is a little closer to me.

THESAURUSES

Tanya Davis, Queer Youth Writing Club Facilitator (she/her)

It was a muggy summer evening and Pride Week had just ended, which means we had all been super gay for about seven days, waving flags, amidst friends, safer than usual. I was scheduled to lead a workshop for the Queer Youth Writing Club, and I was nervous. I was nervous because teaching is intimidating to me, as are groups. And, of course, I wanted everyone at writing club to think I was cool (I already knew *they* were cool).

My workshop was about thesauruses, so I was either off to a very cool start or a very nerdy one, depending on how you feel about thesauruses (thesauri?). I figured, since it was for a writing group, this kind of workshop was fitting. And, if it wasn't immediately cool, maybe it would trickle down and be cool later, when someone was searching for a perfect word and remembered that used copy of *Roget's A-Z*.

Earlier that day, I had cleared all Charlottetown thrift stores of their thesaurus collections, which was basically the most fun I'd ever had thrift shopping. I carried the books into the Haviland Club, imagining their musty pages feeling right at home in the walls of that old building. I stacked them on the shelf and felt my nervousness shift slightly towards excitement. So many synonyms.

I decided to give a workshop about thesauruses because I wanted to talk about the construction blocks of writing—words. I wanted to talk about words because they've been a haven of mine since I was a young writer, overwhelmed by the world around me but steady at my desk, pen in hand and thesaurus within reach. My desk, ironically, was in a closet. A literal closet in the basement next to my bedroom. I didn't mind, and I was some years away from seeing the symbolism in that (a bit sad, a bit hilarious). What I did see, alone in my teenage writing zone, was how a word could open a secret door, how it could illuminate an unfamiliar

ARE WE FRIENDS NOW?

passageway and lead me somewhere new. I saw, too, that a word could cut deep and immediate, that it could injure as well as heal. I learned that words were powerful and needed to be wielded with care.

The more I wrote—in my closet and then, eventually, out of it—the more I understood that words also had their shortcomings, just like people, and that trying to describe something was as hard as trying to describe myself. I needed the elasticity of synonyms, and the freedom of change. I honoured my thesaurus like a queer leader of sorts, a representative of my worldview that there are endless ways to be. It became a beacon, lighting a path I could follow through the limiting hallways of high school.

I've been carrying a thesaurus in my backpack ever since. I have one in front of me here on my desk (by a window now, always). It's a practical reference book that improves our vocabulary; it's a powerful talisman that expands our world.

I'm not sure I said all that in the workshop I gave at writing club. I'm not sure I could have. Maybe my nerves were overactivated by so many thesauri in one room, or so many cool young people who lived with a flair I couldn't find when I was their age—free to express, free to explore a certain synonym one day and a different one the next.

Of course, it's more complicated than that—freedom is tenuous and disproportionate, which is one of the reasons Queer Youth Writing Club is a necessary space, and one of the reasons I was grateful to be there, amidst friends, safer than usual. On that muggy summer evening, I tried to convey the potential of a thesaurus, its ability to enhance language and open minds. At minimum, every participant got to hold one and flip through, skimming synonyms wayward and perfect. I hope they also stumbled upon a curious question, a dazzling definition, a rousing invitation sent by a humble word.

THE QUEEN OF NOTHING

Hayden Little (she/her)

From her icy throne
compiled of nothing but stone and bone
She sits idly

There is nothing she cannot acquire
Nothing she can't conquer

And yet she shifts

And yet there's a sway in the way she gazes out
A complex longing
that no one mind can comprehend

But how can one set down power
for something as brief as a kiss?

VOLUME 2: PAPER FENCE

Seth C.G. (he/him)

Somewhere in the unknown
I lay with my face on the floor

Though I think I'm alone
The shadows always stand at my door

I'm looking for the tiniest light
And I scream in dragon's breath

I'm looking for a reason to fight
I feel that overwhelming sense of death

A plastic house with a paper fence
I guess that shows how weak I am

I look around, it's no contest
But through the lens I'm a hologram

And the gods strike me down
A display to the others

But I never had a crown
So why would they bother?

BLACKOUT POETRY

Evan Currie (he/him)

love your body,

if this is

enough for you

surgeries

there's no other place you can go.

you need to love parts of

you

you'll need surgeries.

various surgeries,

body,

change,

precise

effective

surgeries.

~ Excerpt from: *The Anxiety Book for Trans People*, by Freija Benson

WiNGED KiNG

Seth C.G. (he/him)

In my dreams I saw
Mountains edging the sky
Pizzicato points of brown
In a simple blue landscape

There was a lake
And if you stared into it
A bird was destined to fly past you
Maybe it was a phoenix
Who was destined to finish
But would come back, somehow

I saw clouds
But not clouds of candy
Clouds of vision and passion
Simple legato to compliment
That edge of the mountains

Over the horizon there was a crater
Something was within the crater
It was a Winged King
The King knew the skies too well

It caught one glimpse of me and embarked
A single stroke of red to add to the canvas

EVERAPPLE
Hayden Little (she/her)

They feed her rotting flowers and molding mice
Dress her in strips of stolen curtain
and kiss her with berry-stained lips

"How pretty you look, like this."
They churr
"But not so lovely as you all."
She says

Nonsense they hum
adorning her with rusting jewels of beetles and blackbirds
who buzz with fluttering howls when she sways

They shriek in delight as she trips
kicking leaves into her face while she marvels at them
Every busted vein glitters like gold
so long as she stays full

WHY DO i HAVE THE MOST USELESS LUCK?

Mnemosyne Tabangin (she/they)

Look, I know I always open up discussions with a complaint or some whine or whatever, but I can't help it. I guess that makes me pathetic, but I'll call it... uh... my own misery?

Whatever, back to the case in point. My luck is useless and you might be wondering why. Well, it's just useless I guess. My luck only seems to exist in the most impractical of situations. Way back in my original time, when I only struck gold when it came for perfect rain to feed the crops, or I spotted some special-coloured bird. Yeah, LUCKY, but did it help me not get chosen to go on missions? Did it help me avoid the most horrific monsters I've seen? Did it help me when I tripped and fell into the future? No. No it didn't.

Nowadays, whatever 'good' luck I have is wasted on games or even the stupid gambling sessions Caspara brings me to because she KNOWS my horrid luck. The games I play where it's ring based? I get too bored because I keep getting those ultra rank items or firestars. My accounts are disgusting in that sense. My horrible luck?

Happening right now.

My body is hugged on the wall, my back pressed into some wall in the shadows of a random alleyway. My eyes are wide as I sit still, sticking to the wall for comfort.

(to be continued...)

UNTiTLED

Rachel Collier, Queer Youth Writing Club Facilitator (she/her)

A writer, a writer
I want to be

Ink on paper
Could set me free

Fairies and goblins
Punchlines and hooks

Let me tell you
We've got a book

Share, shape, shift, grow
We should really write this down

In space with peers?
I'd rather clown

Ink alone
Won't set me free

Try a room full of friends
who see I'm me

And a community who celebrates
the person I'd like to be.

POEM #3

Elizabeth Morrison (she/her)

Touch.

Time.

Gifts.

Affirmations.

Actions.

The languages of love, for all but I.

The only language of love that penetrates the boundaries of my heart belongs solely to you and me.

Spoken in subtle glances from across a crowded room.

Fingers intertwining without so much as a look.

Arms and legs tangled under the cover of night.

The security of our comfortable silences.

The softest of hands caressing mine.

Your hand pressed against my skin in the most vulnerable of moments.

Never truly knowing where my body ends and yours begins.

It is forever and always the language of my soul,

And when every word, thought, and memory fades from my ever-longing brain,

Our language, our love, will be all that remains.

Until we are alone together at the bittersweet end

Of our eternity spent in minutes.

ARE WE FRIENDS NOW?

A THANK YOU...

To the 2SLGBTQ+ youth who contributed wholeheartedly to this book at every step of the way. This book was made by you, for you, and the adults involved are simply lucky to be a part of it.

To the volunteers (in no particular order): Rachel Collier, Tanya Davis, Austen Clayton, Hal Atwood, Molly Williams, Beck Aurell, Dave Stewart, Robin Sutherland, Dana Doucette, Katrina Cristall, Evelyn Bradley, and Rachel Bartlett. You all gave so selflessly to this book and we cannot say enough how much we appreciate you.

To each and every facilitator, guest speaker, and contributor to this project who shared their knowledge and life experiences so generously with our youth group.

To our project editor Tom Ryan, who went so far above and beyond what was expected to bring this all together that it inspired the rest of the team.

To Acorn Press Canada for stepping up and helping us publish the book that we believe can make a difference in people's lives.

To the PEERS Alliance and the PEI Writers' Guild organizations for giving their time, energy, love, and resources to such a worthy project.

To Shawn Hogan from the PEI Writers' Guild, for letting the youth tease you mercilessly and for all of your hard work and love for this project that made it what it is today.

To Vanessa Bradley from PEERS Alliance for, well, for being you. Your contributions to this project are too many to list and without you involved it could not have been possible.

To the PEI Alliance for Mental Well-Being for funding this project and giving us the space and support needed to get this book off the ground.

BiOGRAPHiES
(in Haiku and Mad Lib format)

VANESSA BRADLEY (SHE/HER)

<u>Vanessa</u> loves <u>her wife</u>
   NAME   NOUN

Enjoys <u>howling at the moon</u>
            VERB

and despises <u>being burned at the stake</u>.
            NOUN

SETH C.G (HE/HiM)

Believes that all life
Is here for a great reason
We just don't know it

RACHEL COLLiER (SHE/HER)

Rachel Collier loves fire
Enjoys soaking up sun
Despises The Cold

EVAN CURRIE (HE/HIM)

Evan loves mermen
NAME   NOUN

Enjoys digging graves
         VERB

and despises confrontation.
         NOUN

TANYA DAVIS (SHE/HER)

lives in the country

writes words, plays tunes, swims often

grows food and pats cats

SHAWN HOGAN (HE/HIM)

Shawn loves George (his dog)
NAME   NOUN

Enjoys throwing his hat
         VERB

and despises being compared to Tom.
         NOUN

OAK LEBLANC (THEY/HE)

Oak loves trees
NAME NOUN

Enjoys eating fruity fruit gummies
   VERB

and despises termites.
   NOUN

ANACLARA LEYENAAR (SHE/THEY)

Anaclara loves butterfly emojis
NAME NOUN

Enjoys procrastinating
   VERB

and despises imperfection in her writing.
   NOUN

HAYDEN LiTTLE (SHE/HER)

Hayden loves vintage dresses
NAME NOUN

Enjoys listening to Aurora
   VERB

and despises the title of the book.
   NOUN

ELIZABETH MORRISON (SHE/HER)

a lover of stars,
a dreamer of worlds afar,
romantic at heart.

ROISIN MULLEN (SHE/HE/THEY)

makes jewelry and art
and her roller derby name
is Rebel Rebel

HEATHER ROSS (SHE/HER)

Likes looking at life
Through the lens of time and love
then writing it down

TOM RYAN (HE/HIM)

<u>Tom</u> loves <u>his husband</u>
  NAME   NOUN

Enjoys <u>editing books</u>
        VERB

and despises <u>cutting off his finger with a gardening shear.</u>
        NOUN

DAVE STEWART (HE/HiM)

<u>Dave</u> loves <u>Dave (his husband)</u>
  NAME   NOUN

Enjoys <u>listening to Aurora</u>
          VERB

and despises <u>the haters and the roaches</u>.
               NOUN

MNEMOSYNE TABANGiN (SHE/THEY)

Very tired and bored
Imagination in dreams,
I am Mnemosyne.

RiVER WATERMAN (THEY/THEM)

River writes her thoughts,
strange, colourful confusion
collaged on paper

MOLLY WiLLiAMS (SHE/HER)

I'm pretty. I'm pretty.
I get prettier everyday—
electric-heart, sun-dance.

Big things
have small beginnings.

From acorn to mighty oak, or in our case, an initial manuscript to a well-crafted book.

Thank you for being part of our onGROWING literary journey.

Thank you!

ACORNPRESS

Thanks for reading!

ACORNPRESS

acornpresscanada.com